BRITAIN IN OLD PHOTOGRAPHS

BASINGSTOKE
PAST & PRESENT

TIM EVANS

SUTTON PUBLISHING LIMITED

Sutton Publishing Limited
Phoenix Mill · Thrupp · Stroud
Gloucestershire · GL5 2BU

First published 1997

Cover photographs: *front*: London Street, 1937; Wote Street, viewed from the town hall, present day.

British Library Cataloguing in Publication Data
A catalogue record for this book is available from the British Library.

ISBN 0-7509-1626-5

Typeset in 10/12 Perpetua.
Typesetting and origination by Sutton Publishing Limited.
Printed in Great Britain by Ebenezer Baylis, Worcester.

ACKNOWLEDGEMENTS

Photographs taken in 1997 by Tina Oliver and Chris Surtell at Studio twenty sixty-five.
Archive photographs from the Hampshire County Museum Service.

INTRODUCTION

A visitor to Basingstoke may be forgiven for thinking that amid the hustle and bustle of this thriving modern town and centre of commerce there would be little to remind us of old Basingstoke, of the town our grandparents knew 100 years ago.

Many could also be forgiven for thinking that Basingstoke had any past at all. Over the last thirty years the relentless march of progress has left an indelible mark on the town. Contemporary office high-rises and 1970s post-modernist architecture have replaced many of the old eighteenth- and nineteenth-century timber-framed cottages, turn-of-the-century shop fronts and late Victorian terraces that used to predominate.

Having survived almost intact the rigours of two world wars, it was bewildering to many in the 1960s to see the greatest structural devastation of the town taking place at the hands of many town planners and architects. As a consequence, Basingstoke today is a mere shadow of its former self, of the town that stood for so many hundreds of years unaffected by the passage of time. To the uninformed visitor, Basingstoke today may appear to be a new town; yet if you know where to look, the remnants of the past are never far away, and can be clearly seen.

This book uses images of the past and the present to draw out that comparison, and remind us that the past is really all around us, if we only know where to look.

Tim Evans
Curator of the Willis Museum
Basingstoke

Chapel Street, looking towards the railway bridge, *c.* 1930. It derives its name from the Holy Ghost Chapel that stands nearby, and was originally known as Whitewaye. The old timber-framed cottages on the right date from the seventeenth century.

Junction Road, situated between Chapel Street and Station Hill, *c.* 1920. The terraced properties date from the 1870s.

Station Hill, 1903. Originally built across open fields to connect Lower Wote Street with 'new' station, it was the steepest road in the town.

Station Hill, 1903. The station was opened in 1839 and the line ran from London to Basingstoke, reaching Southampton in 1840. Note the horse and carriage 'parked' by the wall.

Station Hill, 1903. This photograph was taken while the new L & SWR station was being built. On the left is the old Junction Inn.

Saint Mary's Church, Eastrop, *c.* 1910. This church was situated at the junction with Goat Lane and Dark Lane. Originally it was built for the lord of the manor and its earliest known rector was Henry Le Fleming in 1274. It was the smallest church in Hampshire until 1865 and remained thatched until 1886. Eastrop continued as a separate parish until 1892.

London Road looking east, c. 1930. The White Hart Inn, seen on the right, is over two hundred and fifty years old and has probably only survived the ravages of time because of its remoteness from the centre of the town.

London Street from Hackwood Road, 1903.

London Road, viewed from London Street, *c.* 1900. The white building on the right with the three dormer windows was, and is, known as Goldings. This building dates from the Tudor period and may originally have been a farmhouse or roadside inn. Some of its influences date from the eighteenth century, particularly the Queen Anne period. Part of the exterior has now been uncovered to reveal some of the original timber framing.

Deane's Almshouses, *c*. 1900. These buildings date from 1607 and are named after Sir James Deane with whose bequest they were built. Originally there was a pig market situated at the front, but it was eventually moved after continual complaints about the smell.

The Lamb Inn, at the junction of Hackwood Road and Cliddesden Road, *c.* 1910. This was one of many public houses in Basingstoke with associated animal names. Others were the Goat, the Swan, the Pheasant, the Black Cow, the Eagle and the Falcon.

Cliddesden Road, showing Beaconsfield Road junction, *c.* 1930.

Cliddesden Road, 1936. The cottages on the right date from the mid- to late nineteenth century.

Fairfields School, *c.* 1900. The school dates from 1888 and was built on the site of an old fairground, used for the local sheepfair, that was granted to the town in the Enclosure Award of 1786, hence the name of the school.

Bounty Road, looking west, *c.* 1920. This road was originally known as Southern Road until renamed after May's Bounty, the cricket ground gifted by Colonel John May.

Brinklets Hall in Winchester Road, looking towards Winton Square, 1905.

Winton Square and Winchester Road, viewed from Winchester Street, 1905.

Winchester Street, looking east towards the market-place, at the time of the Silver Jubilee, 1937.

The Plaza Cinema, at the top of Sarum Hill/Winton Square, 1937. Seen here decorated for the Silver Jubilee, it was originally built as a drill hall in 1883. In 1925 it became the Pavilion Dance Hall and then the Plaza Cinema in 1933. In 1955 it became the Basingstoke Co-operative Society furnishing store, continuing in this role until demolition in 1981.

The lower end of Flaxfield Road viewed from Worting Road, *c.* 1930. This road derives its name from 'Le Flexacre', a fourteenth-century name.

Worting Road, looking west, *c.* 1910.
Originally known as Upper Way, Worting
Road is associated with settlements dating
back as far as the Belgic Invasion in 55 BC
and the Roman occupation.

Queen Mary's Grammar School, Worting Road, *c.* 1930. The origins of this school date back to the Middle Ages and the brotherhood of the Holy Ghost Chapel, known to have been in existence in the thirteenth century. The school building dates from 1855, but was not used after 1940 when the school moved to larger premises in Vyne Road. Until its recent demolition the building was being used by Basingstoke College of Technology.

Deep Lane, viewed from Worting Road, *c.* 1920. This lane probably derived its name from its origins as a deeply rutted cart track before any buildings had been erected in the area in the sixteenth century.

Worting Road cemetery entrance, *c*. 1900.

The Waterworks Pumping Station at West Ham, 1906. Before the opening of the Pumping Station in 1880, local people in the town had to draw their water from wells. With no formal disposal of sewage at that time, except local cesspits and the local River Loddon, pollution of the local water was a real hazard. The Pumping Station brought piped water into the town for the first time, drawn through street pumps, and this greatly reduced the problem.

Lower Church Street, 1897.

Saint Michael's Church, Lower Church Street, 1903. The church dates back to the Saxon period and in 1086 it was held by Walter, Bishop of Hereford, chaplain to Queen Edgitha. In 1233 Peter de Repibus, Bishop of Winchester, gave it to the Priory of Selbourne, along with Basing. During the Civil War, horses and gunpowder were stored there, and during the Second World War some of the windows were blown out by a stick of bombs falling in Church Square. Some of the walls were pitted by bomb blasts and this can still be clearly seen today.

Church Street, 1910.

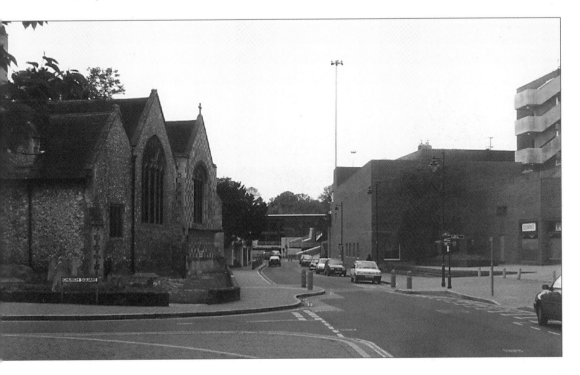

Church Square, *c.* 1920. A number of these properties were demolished in August 1940, when German bombers flew over the town and dropped a stick of bombs on the square.

Cross Street, looking towards New Street and Flaxfield Road, *c.* 1910. This area is best known for the Blue Coat School, which is just out of this picture on the right.

The corner of New Street and Flaxfield Road, *c.* 1900. New Street is a corruption of the name Stew Street that ran from Cow Cross Lane, later to be called Cross Lane, to Allen Lane, later to be called Victoria Street.

New Street, looking towards Winchester Street, 1901.

New Street, looking down towards Cross Street and Flaxfield Street, 1880.

New Street, viewed from Winchester Street, 1920.

Winchester Street, viewed from the New Street and Victoria Street junction, *c.* 1890.

Winchester Street, *c*. 1920. Edgar Lanham acquired the store in 1914 from Thomas Burberry; this is the 'Emporium' built after the great fire of 1905. In its time Lanham's sold nearly every household item that was needed.

The Crown Inn, Winchester Street, *c.* 1900.

Winchester Street, 1880.

Winchester Street, viewed from the market-place, 1880. Behind Freeman, Hardy & Willis were the Assembly Rooms, where it is believed Jane Austen came to dances.

The market-place, looking down Winchester Street, *c.* 1880.

The market-place, *c.* 1900.

The market-place, looking down Winchester Street.

The top of Church Street on the market-place, 1880. Note the old Ship Inn.

Church Street, viewed from the market-place, *c.* 1920. The name Church Street may well predate Saint Michael's Church and probably refers to the track that originally led to the Holy Ghost Chapel and Chapel Street.

Church Street during the Silver Jubilee celebrations, 1937. Note Longley's shop on the left.

Church Street, 1880. Note the Black Boy Hotel on the left, now called the Hop Leaf. The hotel's emblem used to be a statue of a small Negro boy standing beside a tobacco coil, which is now to be found in the Willis Museum. This would certainly denote the sale of tobacco, as well as beverages, but may also have been an association with the slave trade. Note also the little dustpan sign; a similar sign is still visible today in Longley's window.

The market-place, 1903. The original alleyway or 'twittern' that runs beside McDonald's can be seen below.

London Street, looking towards Hackwood Road, 1903. Note the earth road; these were made of impacted flint and earth. Women and children would be employed by local farmers as 'stone pickers' to clear flints from their fields. These would then be brought into town by the cart load and workmen would break then into small fragments.

Mark Lane, off London Street, 1900.

London Street, looking towards the market-place, 1890. Note the Red Lion Hotel on the right.

London Street, looking towards Hackwood Road junction, 1890. Note the Anchor Inn and 'Strange's Aldermarston Ales & Stouts'.

London Street, looking towards the market-place, 1880. The large building on the right is the United Reform Church built in 1800. It was extended in 1839, 1860 and again very recently.

London Street, looking towards Hackwood Road, 1890.

Celebrations for the Silver Jubilee in London Street, 1937.

The corner of Wote Street and London Street, 1870 (above). This is one of the earliest known photographs of Basingstoke. Note what appear to be piles of flints in the foreground used for road repairs. The picture below was taken in about 1950.

The Wote Street/London Street corner.

The town hall on the market-place, 1907. The earliest recorded town hall or mote hall in Basingstoke dates from the sixteenth century. The existing building dates from 1832 and was built on the site of the Royal Oak Inn at a cost of £10,000. The clock tower, erected by Colonel John May to celebrate Queen Victoria's Diamond Jubilee, replaced the original tower, but was taken down in 1961 as it was deemed to be unsafe. The building had ceased to be the town hall by 1981 and was taken over as the Willis Museum.

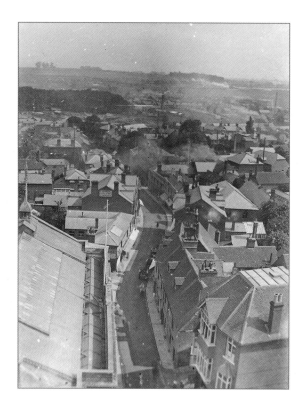

Wote Street, viewed from the town hall
clock tower, 1950.

The Grand Cinema, following the fire, *c.* 1925. Built originally as a corn exchange in 1865, it was used by farmers from all over Hampshire and Berkshire. Although burnt down in 1925, it was rebuilt and has been a roller-skating rink, home for the local fire brigade, and is currently the Haymarket Theatre.

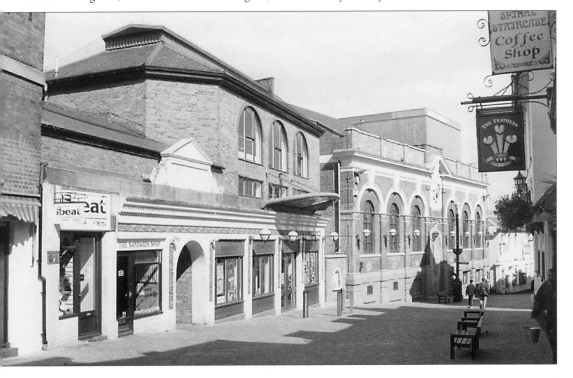

Wote Street, 1910. The origin of this name is puzzling. During the sixteenth century it was known as Ote Street and more recently as Oat Street. One theory suggests it may be derived from the word mote from mote hall, an early name for a meeting hall on the market-place.

Silver Jubilee celebrations in Wote Street, 1937.

Brook Street, looking towards Reading Road and Basing Road. On the right is the Wharf, originally belonging to Basingstoke Canal, which later became a timber yard with saw mills owned by Mr E.C. White. Also seen is the Engineer Arms, named after the engineering firm of Wallis & Stevens, whose men used the pub at lunchtimes.